THIS BOOK BELONGS TO

1

COLOR TEST

3

TRY PAINTING YOURSELF

7

TRY PAINTING YOURSELF

9

TRY PAINTING YOURSELF

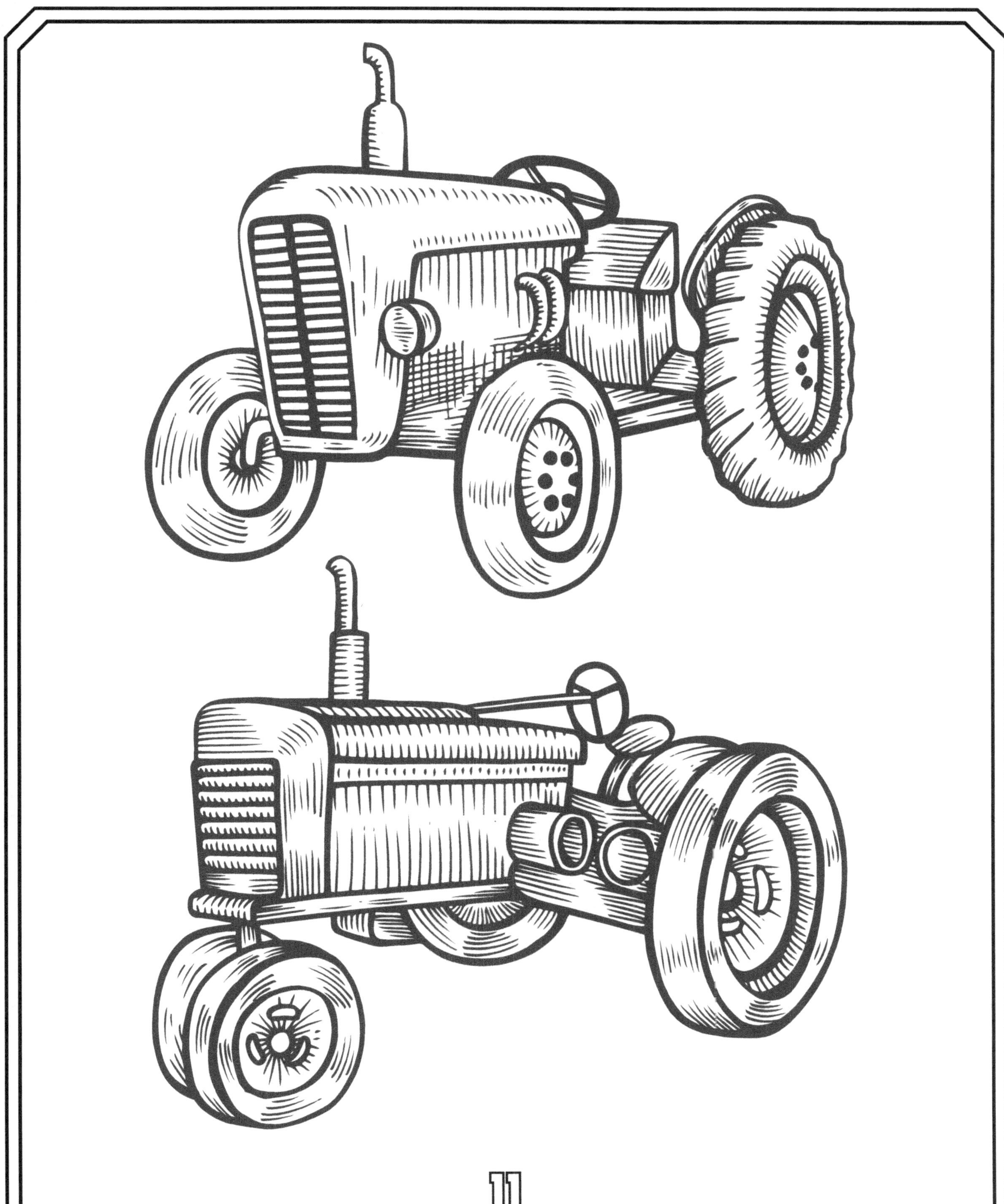

TRY PAINTING YOURSELF

13

TRY PAINTING YOURSELF

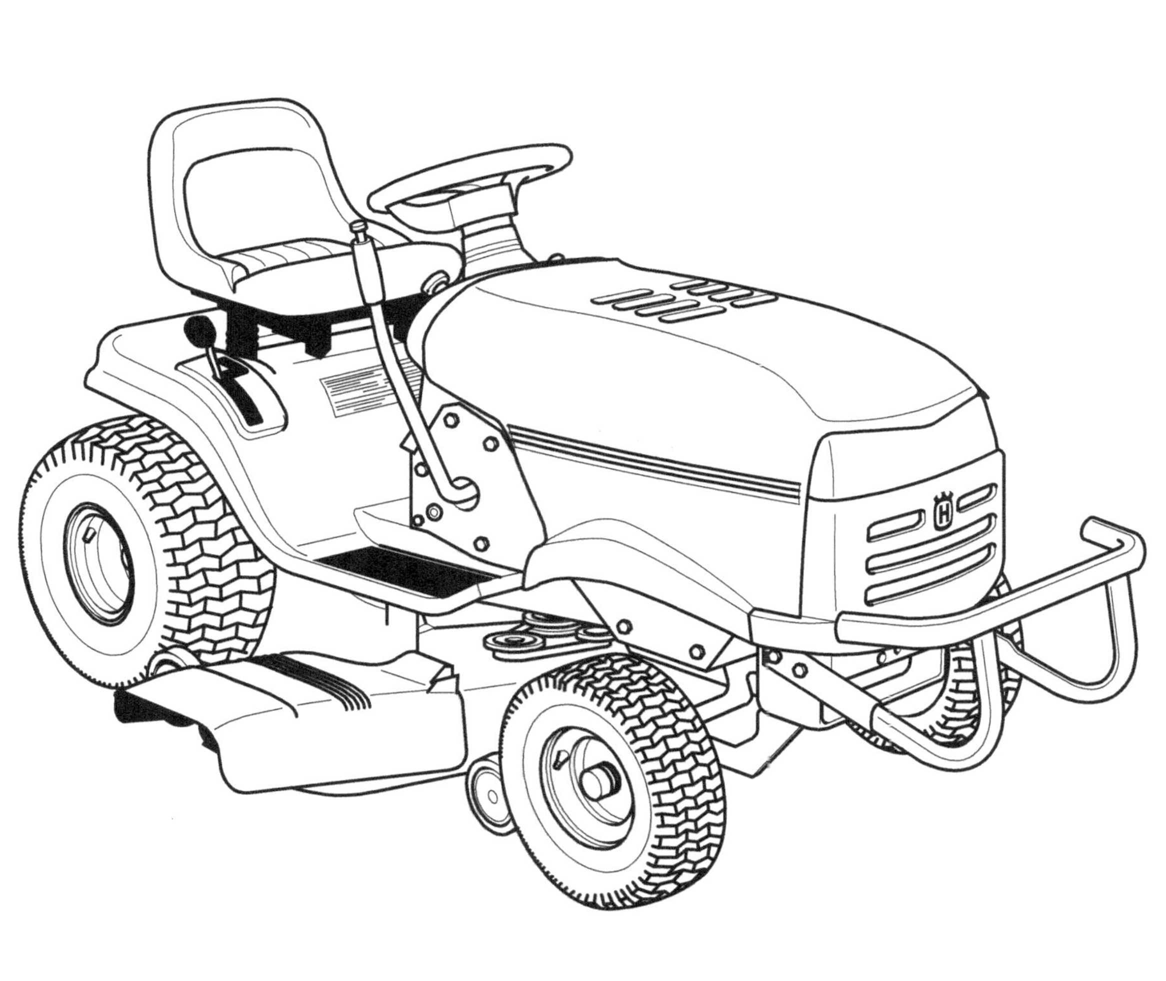

TRY PAINTING YOURSELF

17

TRY PAINTING YOURSELF

19

TRY PAINTING YOURSELF

TRY PAINTING YOURSELF

23

TRY PAINTING YOURSELF

25

TRY PAINTING YOURSELF

FARM
27

TRY PAINTING YOURSELF

29

TRY PAINTING YOURSELF

31

TRY PAINTING YOURSELF

33

TRY PAINTING YOURSELF

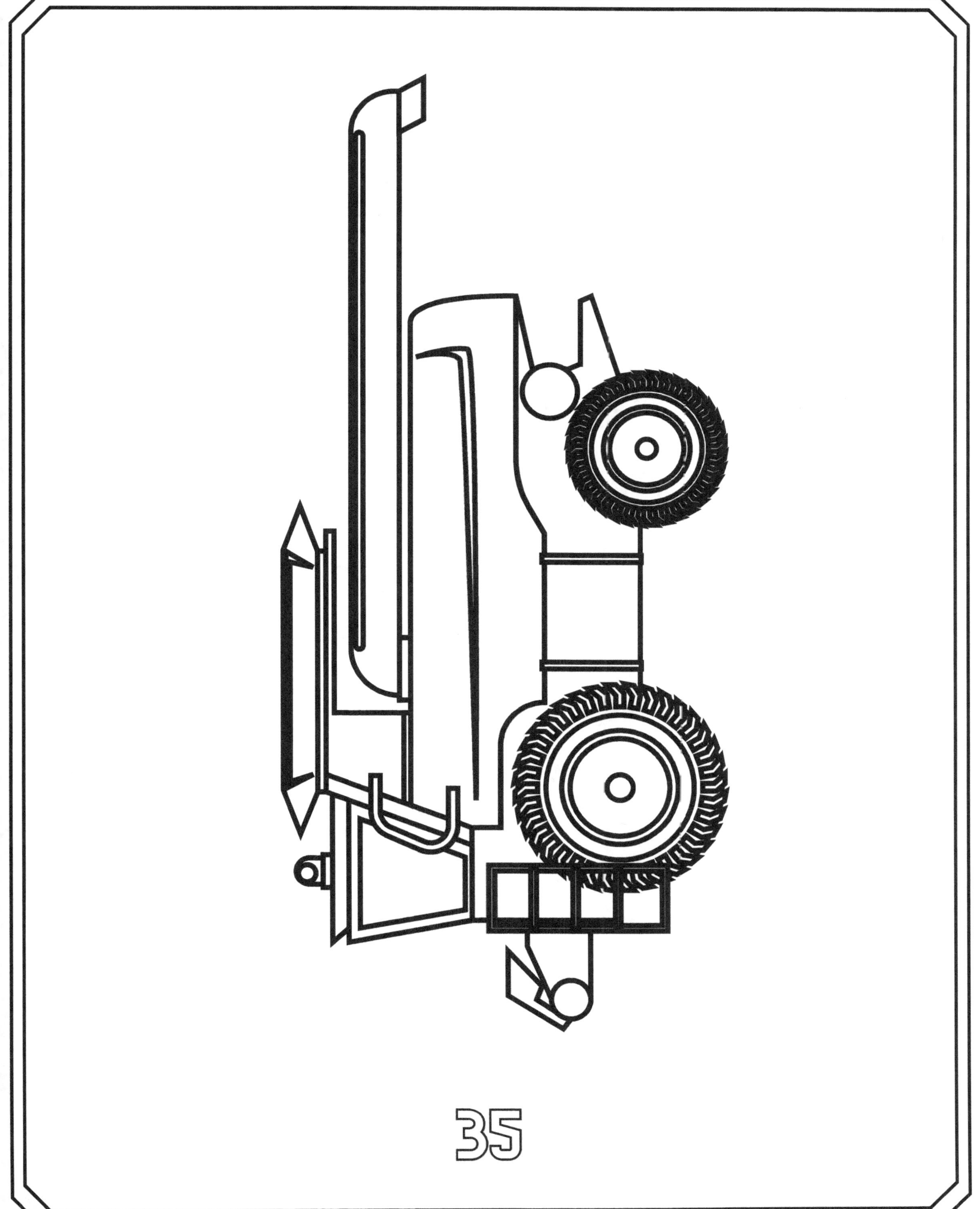

35

TRY PAINTING YOURSELF

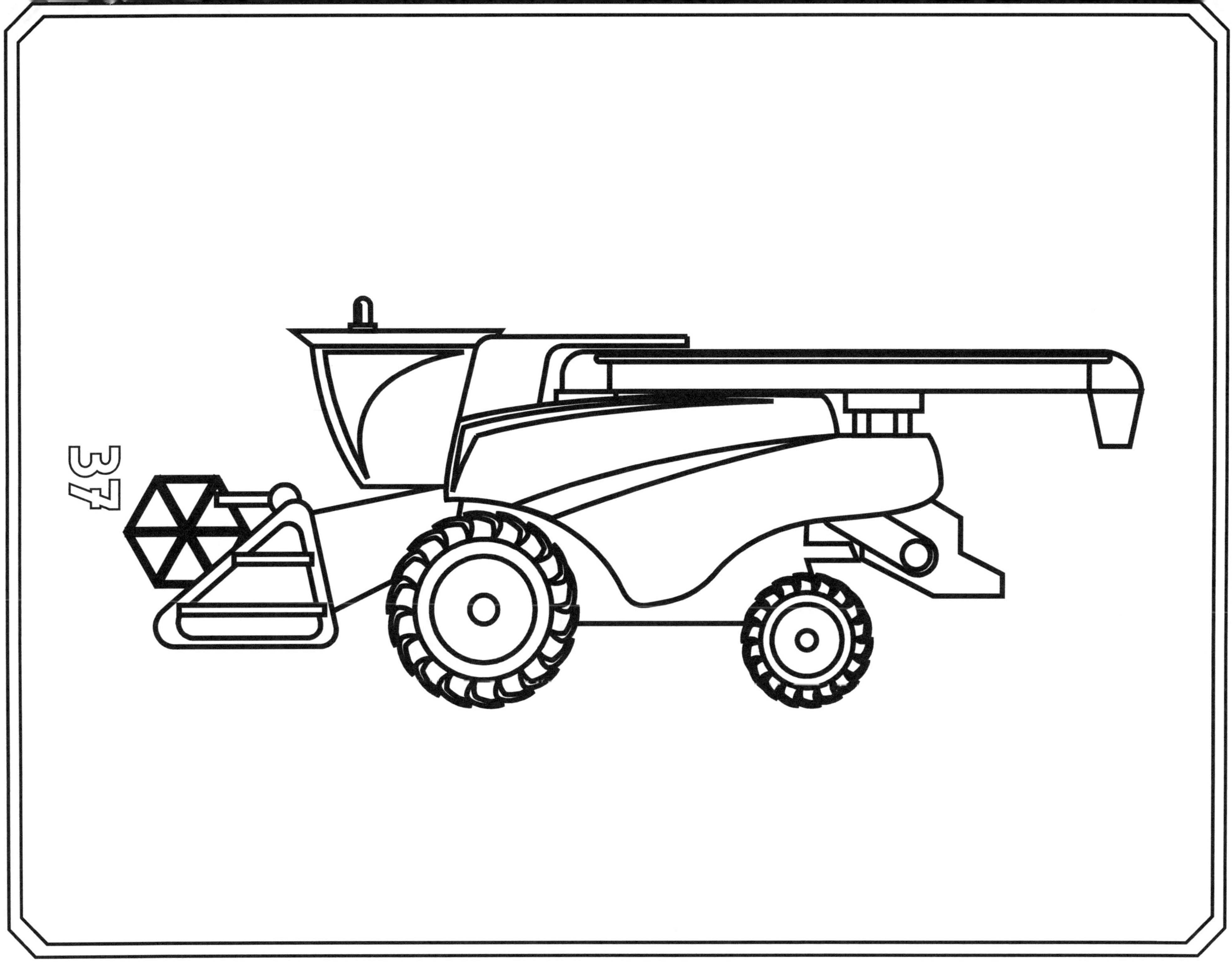

37

TRY PAINTING YOURSELF

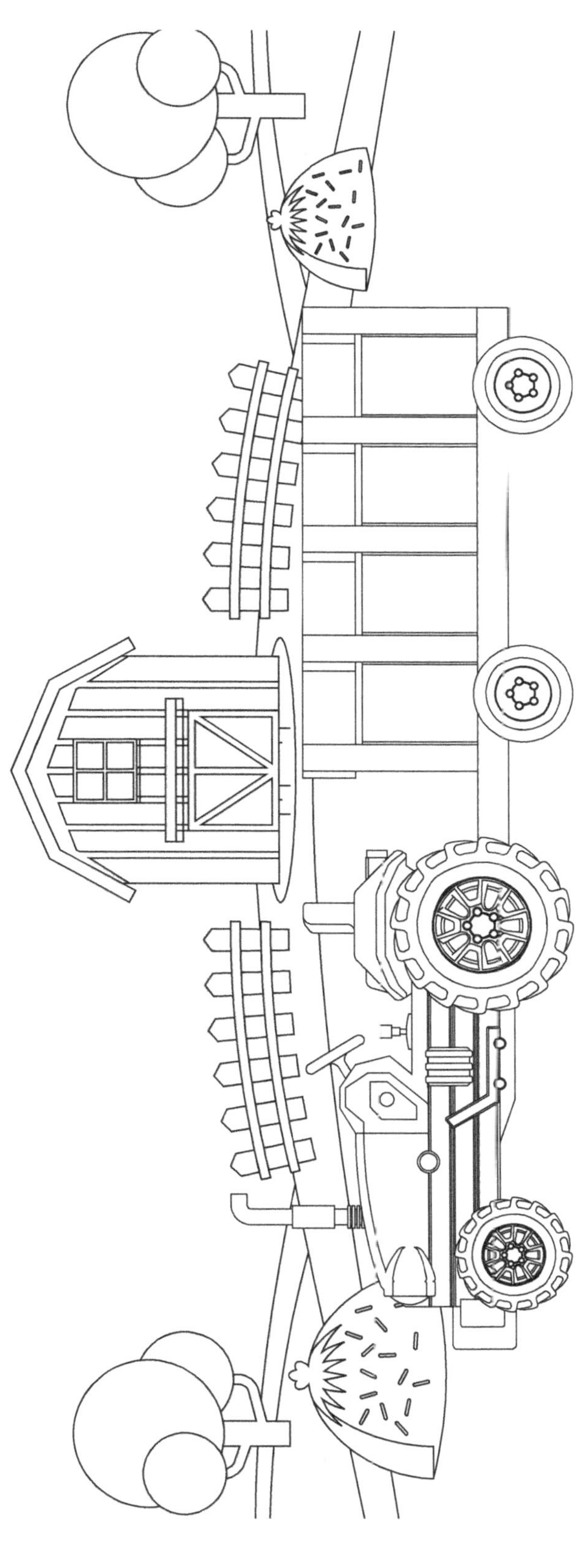

39

TRY PAINTING YOURSELF

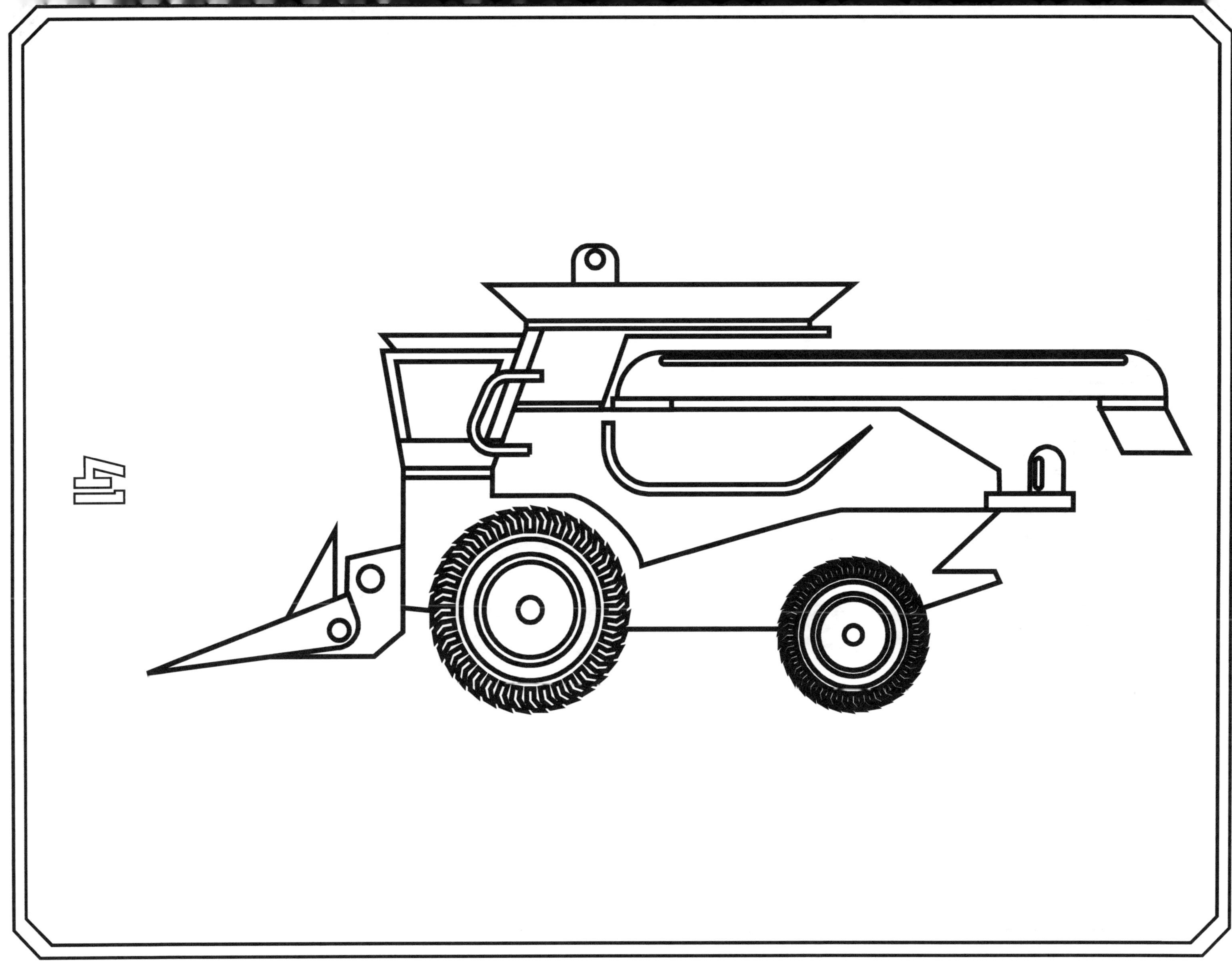

41

TRY PAINTING YOURSELF

43

TRY PAINTING YOURSELF

THANK YOU

<a href="https://www.vecteezy.com/free-vector/combine">Combine Vectors by Vecteezy</a>
<a href="https://www.vecteezy.com/free-vector/tractor">Tractor Vectors by Vecteezy</a>
<a href="https://www.vecteezy.com/free-vector/tractor">Tractor Vectors by Vecteezy</a>
<a href="https://www.vecteezy.com/free-vector/nature">Nature Vectors by Vecteezy</a>
<a href="https://www.vecteezy.com/free-vector/tractor">Tractor Vectors by Vecteezy</a>
<a href="https://www.vecteezy.com/free-vector/house-sketch">House Sketch Vectors by Vecteezy</a>
<a href="https://www.vecteezy.com/free-vector/tractor">Tractor Vectors by Vecteezy</a>
<a href="https://www.vecteezy.com/free-vector/hayride">Hayride Vectors by Vecteezy</a>
<a href="https://www.vecteezy.com/free-vector/tractor">Tractor Vectors by Vecteezy</a>
<a href="https://www.vecteezy.com/free-vector/countryside">Countryside Vectors by Vecteezy</a>
<a href="https://www.vecteezy.com/free-vector/farm">Farm Vectors by Vecteezy</a>
<a href="https://www.vecteezy.com/free-vector/farm-equipment">Farm Equipment Vectors by Vecteezy</a>
<a href="https://www.vecteezy.com/free-vector/tractor">Tractor Vectors by Vecteezy</a>
<a href="https://www.vecteezy.com/free-vector/farm">Farm Vectors by Vecteezy</a>
<a href="https://www.vecteezy.com/free-vector/farm">Farm Vectors by Vecteezy</a>

www.ingramcontent.com/pod-product-compliance
Lightning Source LLC
Chambersburg PA
CBHW081323250726
48662CB00008B/2724